'It's a dreadful
thing to yie
but resist n
Lay my pri
bare to the
blows of rui
That's drea
too.'

SOPHOCLES
Born 496 BC, Colonus, Greece
Died *c.* 406 BC, Athens, Greece

The play was written in its original Greek in or before
441 BC and is taken from *The Three Theban Plays*,
translated by Robert Fagles.

SOPHOCLES IN PENGUIN CLASSICS
The Three Theban Plays
Electra and Other Plays

SOPHOCLES

Antigone

Translated by
Robert Fagles

PENGUIN BOOKS

PENGUIN CLASSICS

Published by the Penguin Group
Penguin Books Ltd, 80 Strand, London WC2R 0RL, England
Penguin Group (USA) Inc., 375 Hudson Street, New York, New York 10014, USA
Penguin Group (Canada), 90 Eglinton Avenue East, Suite 700, Toronto, Ontario,
Canada M4P 2Y3 (a division of Pearson Penguin Canada Inc.)
Penguin Ireland, 25 St Stephen's Green, Dublin 2, Ireland
(a division of Penguin Books Ltd)
Penguin Group (Australia), 707 Collins Street, Melbourne, Victoria 3008, Australia
(a division of Pearson Australia Group Pty Ltd)
Penguin Books India Pvt Ltd, 11 Community Centre, Panchsheel Park,
New Delhi – 110 017, India
Penguin Group (NZ), 67 Apollo Drive, Rosedale, Auckland 0632, New Zealand
(a division of Pearson New Zealand Ltd)
Penguin Books (South Africa) (Pty) Ltd, Block D, Rosebank Office Park,
181 Jan Smuts Avenue, Parktown North, Gauteng 2193, South Africa

Penguin Books Ltd, Registered Offices: 80 Strand, London WC2R 0RL, England

www.penguin.com

This edition published in Penguin Classics 2015
002

Translation copyright © Robert Fagles, 1982, 1984
The moral right of the translator has been asserted

Set in 7.25/10 pt Baskerville 10 Pro
Typeset by Jouve (UK), Milton Keynes
Printed in Great Britain by Clays Ltd, St Ives plc

A CIP catalogue record for this book is available from the British Library

ISBN: 978-0-141-39770-2

www.greenpenguin.co.uk

Characters

ANTIGONE
daughter of Oedipus and Jocasta

ISMENE
sister of Antigone

A CHORUS
of old Theban citizens and their LEADER

CREON
king of Thebes, uncle of Antigone and Ismene

A SENTRY

HAEMON
son of Creon and Eurydice

TIRESIAS
a blind prophet

A MESSENGER

EURYDICE
wife of Creon

Guards, attendants, and a boy

ANTIGONE:

My own flesh and blood – dear sister, dear Ismene,
how many griefs our father Oedipus handed down!
Do you know one, I ask you, one grief
that Zeus will not perfect for the two of us
while we still live and breathe? There's nothing,
no pain – our lives are pain – no private shame,
no public disgrace, nothing I haven't seen
in your griefs and mine. And now this:
an emergency decree, they say, the Commander
has just now declared for all of Thebes.
What, haven't you heard? Don't you see?
The doom reserved for enemies
marches on the ones we love the most.

ISMENE:

Not I, I haven't heard a word, Antigone.
Nothing of loved ones,
no joy or pain has come my way, not since
the two of us were robbed of our two brothers,
both gone in a day, a double blow –
not since the armies of Argos vanished,
just this very night. I know nothing more,
whether our luck's improved or ruin's still to come.

3

ANTIGONE:
I thought so. That's why I brought you out here,
past the gates, so you could hear in private.

ISMENE:
What's the matter? Trouble, clearly . . .
you sound so dark, so grim.

ANTIGONE:
Why not? Our own brothers' burial!
Hasn't Creon graced one with all the rites,
disgraced the other? Eteocles, they say,
has been given full military honors,
rightly so – Creon has laid him in the earth
and he goes with glory down among the dead.
But the body of Polynices, who died miserably –
why, a city-wide proclamation, rumor has it,
forbids anyone to bury him, even mourn him.
He's to be left unwept, unburied, a lovely treasure
for birds that scan the field and feast to their heart's content.

Such, I hear, is the martial law our good Creon
lays down for you and me – yes, me, I tell you –
and he's coming here to alert the uninformed
in no uncertain terms,
and he won't treat the matter lightly. Whoever
disobeys in the least will die, his doom is sealed:
stoning to death inside the city walls!

There you have it. You'll soon show what you are,
worth your breeding, Ismene, or a coward –
for all your royal blood.

ISMENE:
My poor sister, if things have come to this,
who am I to make or mend them, tell me,
what good am I to you?

ANTIGONE: Decide.
Will you share the labor, share the work?

ISMENE:
What work, what's the risk? What do you mean?

ANTIGONE: *Raising her hands.*
Will you lift up his body with these bare hands
and lower it with me?

ISMENE: What? You'd bury him –
when a law forbids the city?

ANTIGONE: Yes!
He is my brother and – deny it as you will –
your brother too.
No one will ever convict me for a traitor.

ISMENE:
So desperate, and Creon has expressly –

ANTIGONE: No,
he has no right to keep me from my own.

ISMENE:
Oh my sister, think –
think how our own father died, hated,
his reputation in ruins, driven on
by the crimes he brought to light himself
to gouge out his eyes with his own hands –
then mother . . . his mother and wife, both in one,
mutilating her life in the twisted noose –
and last, our two brothers dead in a single day,
both shedding their own blood, poor suffering boys,
battling out their common destiny hand-to-hand.

Now look at the two of us, left so alone . . .
think what a death we'll die, the worst of all
if we violate the laws and override
the fixed decree of the throne, its power –

we must be sensible. Remember we are women,
we're not born to contend with men. Then too,
we're underlings, ruled by much stronger hands,
so we must submit in this, and things still worse.

I, for one, I'll beg the dead to forgive me –
I'm forced, I have no choice – I must obey
the ones who stand in power. Why rush to extremes?
It's madness, madness.

ANTIGONE: I won't insist,
no, even if you should have a change of heart,
I'd never welcome you in the labor, not with me.
So, do as you like, whatever suits you best –
I will bury him myself.
And even if I die in the act, that death will be a glory.
I will lie with the one I love and loved by him –
an outrage sacred to the gods! I have longer
to please the dead than please the living here:
in the kingdom down below I'll lie forever.
Do as you like, dishonor the laws
the gods hold in honor.

ISMENE: I'd do them no dishonor . . .
but defy the city? I have no strength for that.

ANTIGONE:
You have your excuses. I am on my way,
I will raise a mound for him, for my dear brother.

ISMENE:
Oh Antigone, you're so rash – I'm so afraid for you!

ANTIGONE:
Don't fear for me. Set your own life in order.

ISMENE:
Then don't, at least, blurt this out to anyone.
Keep it a secret. I'll join you in that, I promise.

ANTIGONE:
Dear god, shout it from the rooftops. I'll hate you
all the more for silence – tell the world!

ISMENE:
So fiery – and it ought to chill your heart.

ANTIGONE:
I know I please where I must please the most.

ISMENE:
Yes, if you can, but you're in love with impossibility.

ANTIGONE:
Very well then, once my strength gives out
I will be done at last.

ISMENE: You're wrong from the start,
you're off on a hopeless quest.

ANTIGONE:
If you say so, you will make me hate you,
and the hatred of the dead, by all rights,
will haunt you night and day.
But leave me to my own absurdity, leave me
to suffer this – dreadful thing. I will suffer
nothing as great as death without glory.

Exit to the side.

ISMENE:
Then go if you must, but rest assured,
wild, irrational as you are, my sister,
you are truly dear to the ones who love you.

Withdrawing to the palace.

Enter a CHORUS, *the old citizens
of Thebes, chanting as the sun begins
to rise.*

7

CHORUS:
Glory! – great beam of the sun, brightest of all
that ever rose on the seven gates of Thebes,
   you burn through night at last!
         Great eye of the golden day,
mounting the Dirce's banks you throw him back –
the enemy out of Argos, the white shield, the man of bronze –
he's flying headlong now
       the bridle of fate stampeding him with pain!

    And he had driven against our borders,
    launched by the warring claims of Polynices –
    like an eagle screaming, winging havoc
    over the land, wings of armor
    shielded white as snow,
    a huge army massing,
    crested helmets bristling for assault.

He hovered above our roofs, his vast maw gaping
closing down around our seven gates,
   his spears thirsting for the kill
       but now he's gone, look,
before he could glut his jaws with Theban blood
or the god of fire put our crown of towers to the torch.
He grappled the Dragon none can master – Thebes –
       the clang of our arms like thunder at his back!

    Zeus hates with a vengeance all bravado,
    the mighty boasts of men. He watched them
    coming on in a rising flood, the pride
    of their golden armor ringing shrill –
    and brandishing his lightning
    blasted the fighter just at the goal,
    rushing to shout his triumph from our walls.

Down from the heights he crashed, pounding down on the earth!
And a moment ago, blazing torch in hand –
         mad for attack, ecstatic

he breathed his rage, the storm
  of his fury hurling at our heads!
But now his high hopes have laid him low
and down the enemy ranks the iron god of war
    deals his rewards, his stunning blows – Ares
    rapture of battle, our right arm in the crisis.

    Seven captains marshaled at seven gates
    seven against their equals, gave
    their brazen trophies up to Zeus,
    god of the breaking rout of battle,
    all but two: those blood brothers,
    one father, one mother – matched in rage,
    spears matched for the twin conquest –
    clashed and won the common prize of death.

But now for Victory! Glorious in the morning,
joy in her eyes to meet our joy
  she is winging down to Thebes,
our fleets of chariots wheeling in her wake –
  Now let us win oblivion from the wars,
thronging the temples of the gods
in singing, dancing choirs through the night!
    Lord Dionysus, god of the dance
    that shakes the land of Thebes, now lead the way!

                Enter CREON *from the palace,*
                attended by his guard.

    But look, the king of the realm is coming,
    Creon, the new man for the new day,
    whatever the gods are sending now . . .
    what new plan will he launch?
    Why this, this special session?
    Why this sudden call to the old men
    summoned at one command?

CREON: My countrymen,
the ship of state is safe. The gods who rocked her,
after a long, merciless pounding in the storm,
have righted her once more.

                                    Out of the whole city
I have called you here alone. Well I know,
first, your undeviating respect
for the throne and royal power of King Laius.
Next, while Oedipus steered the land of Thebes,
and even after he died, your loyalty was unshakable,
you still stood by their children. Now then,
since the two sons are dead – two blows of fate
in the same day, cut down by each other's hands,
both killers, both brothers stained with blood –
as I am next in kin to the dead,
I now possess the throne and all its powers.

Of course you cannot know a man completely,
his character, his principles, sense of judgment,
not till he's shown his colors, ruling the people,
making laws. Experience, there's the test.
As I see it, whoever assumes the task,
the awesome task of setting the city's course,
and refuses to adopt the soundest policies
but fearing someone, keeps his lips locked tight,
he's utterly worthless. So I rate him now,
I always have. And whoever places a friend
above the good of his own country, he is nothing:
I have no use for him. Zeus my witness,
Zeus who sees all things, always –

I could never stand by silent, watching destruction
march against our city, putting safety to rout,
nor could I ever make that man a friend of mine
who menaces our country. Remember this:
our country *is* our safety.
Only while she voyages true on course

can we establish friendships, truer than blood itself.
Such are my standards. They make our city great.

Closely akin to them I have proclaimed,
just now, the following decree to our people
concerning the two sons of Oedipus.
Eteocles, who died fighting for Thebes,
excelling all in arms: he shall be buried,
crowned with a hero's honors, the cups we pour
to soak the earth and reach the famous dead.

But as for his blood brother, Polynices,
who returned from exile, home to his father-city
and the gods of his race, consumed with one desire –
to burn them roof to roots – who thirsted to drink
his kinsmen's blood and sell the rest to slavery:
that man – a proclamation has forbidden the city
to dignify him with burial, mourn him at all.
No, he must be left unburied, his corpse
carrion for the birds and dogs to tear,
an obscenity for the citizens to behold!

These are my principles. Never at my hands
will the traitor be honored above the patriot.
But whoever proves his loyalty to the state –
I'll prize that man in death as well as life.

LEADER:
If this is your pleasure, Creon, treating
our city's enemy and our friend this way . . .
The power is yours, I suppose, to enforce it
with the laws, both for the dead and all of us,
the living.

CREON: Follow my orders closely then,
be on your guard.

LEADER: We are too old.
Lay that burden on younger shoulders.

CREON: No, no,
I don't mean the body – I've posted guards already.

LEADER:
What commands for us then? What other service?

CREON:
See that you never side with those who break my orders.

LEADER:
Never. Only a fool could be in love with death.

CREON:
Death is the price – you're right. But all too often
the mere hope of money has ruined many men.

A SENTRY *enters from the side.*

SENTRY: My lord,
I can't say I'm winded from running, or set out
with any spring in my legs either – no sir,
I was lost in thought, and it made me stop, often,
dead in my tracks, wheeling, turning back,
and all the time a voice inside me muttering,
'Idiot, why? You're going straight to your death.'
Then muttering, 'Stopped again, poor fool?
If somebody gets the news to Creon first,
what's to save your neck?'
                                              And so,
mulling it over, on I trudged, dragging my feet,
you can make a short road take forever . . .
but at last, look, common sense won out,
I'm here, and I'm all yours,
and even though I come empty-handed
I'll tell my story just the same, because
I've come with a good grip on one hope,
what will come will come, whatever fate –

CREON:
Come to the point!
What's wrong – why so afraid?

SENTRY:
First, myself, I've got to tell you,
I didn't do it, didn't see who did –
Be fair, don't take it out on me.

CREON:
You're playing it safe, soldier,
barricading yourself from any trouble.
It's obvious, you've something strange to tell.

SENTRY:
Dangerous too, and danger makes you delay
for all you're worth.

CREON:
Out with it – then dismiss!

SENTRY:
All right, here it comes. The body –
someone's just buried it, then run off . . .
sprinkled some dry dust on the flesh,
given it proper rites.

CREON: What?
What man alive would dare –

SENTRY: I've no idea, I swear it.
There was no mark of a spade, no pickaxe there,
no earth turned up, the ground packed hard and dry,
unbroken, no tracks, no wheelruts, nothing,
the workman left no trace. Just at sunup
the first watch of the day points it out –
it was a wonder! We were stunned . . .
a terrific burden too, for all of us, listen:
you can't see the corpse, not that it's buried,

really, just a light cover of road-dust on it,
as if someone meant to lay the dead to rest
and keep from getting cursed.
Not a sign in sight that dogs or wild beasts
had worried the body, even torn the skin.

But what came next! Rough talk flew thick and fast,
guard grilling guard – we'd have come to blows
at last, nothing to stop it; each man for himself
and each the culprit, no one caught red-handed,
all of us pleading ignorance, dodging the charges,
ready to take up red-hot iron in our fists,
go through fire, swear oaths to the gods –
'I didn't do it, I had no hand in it either,
not in the plotting, not the work itself!'

Finally, after all this wrangling came to nothing,
one man spoke out and made us stare at the ground,
hanging our heads in fear. No way to counter him,
no way to take his advice and come through
safe and sound. Here's what he said:
'Look, we've got to report the facts to Creon,
we can't keep this hidden.' Well, that won out,
and the lot fell to me, condemned me,
unlucky as ever, I got the prize. So here I am,
against my will and yours too, well I know –
no one wants the man who brings bad news.

LEADER: My king,
ever since he began I've been debating in my mind,
could this possibly be the work of the gods?

CREON: Stop –
before you make me choke with anger – the gods!
You, you're senile, must you be insane?
You say – why it's intolerable – say the gods
could have the slightest concern for that corpse?
Tell me, was it for meritorious service
they proceeded to bury him, prized him so? The hero

who came to burn their temples ringed with pillars,
their golden treasures – scorch their hallowed earth
and fling their laws to the winds.
Exactly when did you last see the gods
celebrating traitors? Inconceivable!

No, from the first there were certain citizens
who could hardly stand the spirit of my regime,
grumbling against me in the dark, heads together,
tossing wildly, never keeping their necks beneath
the yoke, loyally submitting to their king.
These are the instigators, I'm convinced –
they've perverted my own guard, bribed them
to do their work.
                    Money! Nothing worse
in our lives, so current, rampant, so corrupting.
Money – you demolish cities, root men from their homes,
you train and twist good minds and set them on
to the most atrocious schemes. No limit,
you make them adept at every kind of outrage,
every godless crime – money!
                              Everyone –
the whole crew bribed to commit this crime,
they've made one thing sure at least:
sooner or later they will pay the price.

                    Wheeling on the SENTRY.

                    You –
I swear to Zeus as I still believe in Zeus,
if you don't find the man who buried that corpse,
the very man, and produce him before my eyes,
simple death won't be enough for you,
not till we string you up alive
and wring the immorality out of you.
Then you can steal the rest of your days,
better informed about where to make a killing.
You'll have learned, at last, it doesn't pay

to itch for rewards from every hand that beckons.
Filthy profits wreck most men, you'll see –
they'll never save your life.

SENTRY: Please,
may I say a word or two, or just turn and go?

CREON:
Can't you tell? Everything you say offends me.

SENTRY:
Where does it hurt you, in the ears or in the heart?

CREON:
And who are you to pinpoint my displeasure?

SENTRY:
The culprit grates on your feelings,
I just annoy your ears.

CREON: Still talking?
You talk too much! A born nuisance –

SENTRY: Maybe so,
but I never did this thing, so help me!

CREON: Yes you did –
what's more, you squandered your life for silver!

SENTRY:
Oh it's terrible when the one who does the judging
judges things all wrong.

CREON: Well now,
you just be clever about your judgments –
if you fail to produce the criminals for me,
you'll swear your dirty money brought you pain.

> *Turning sharply, reentering
> the palace.*

SENTRY:
I hope he's found. Best thing by far.
But caught or not, that's in the lap of fortune:
I'll never come back, you've seen the last of me.
I'm saved, even now, and I never thought,
I never hoped –
dear gods, I owe you all my thanks!

Rushing out.

CHORUS: Numberless wonders
terrible wonders walk the world but none the match for man –
that great wonder crossing the heaving gray sea,
                    driven on by the blasts of winter
on through breakers crashing left and right,
   holds his steady course
and the oldest of the gods he wears away –
the Earth, the immortal, the inexhaustible –
as his plows go back and forth, year in, year out
   with the breed of stallions turning up the furrows.

And the blithe, lightheaded race of birds he snares,
the tribes of savage beasts, the life that swarms the depths –
                    with one fling of his nets
woven and coiled tight, he takes them all,
   man the skilled, the brilliant!
He conquers all, taming with his techniques
the prey that roams the cliffs and wild lairs,
training the stallion, clamping the yoke across
   his shaggy neck, and the tireless mountain bull.

And speech and thought, quick as the wind
and the mood and mind for law that rules the city –
   all these he has taught himself
and shelter from the arrows of the frost
when there's rough lodging under the cold clear sky
and the shafts of lashing rain –
                    ready, resourceful man!
                    Never without resources

never an impasse as he marches on the future –
only Death, from Death alone he will find no rescue
but from desperate plagues he has plotted his escapes.

Man the master, ingenious past all measure
past all dreams, the skills within his grasp –
   he forges on, now to destruction
now again to greatness. When he weaves in
the laws of the land, and the justice of the gods
that binds his oaths together
        he and his city rise high –
           but the city casts out
that man who weds himself to inhumanity
thanks to reckless daring. Never share my hearth
never think my thoughts, whoever does such things.

Enter ANTIGONE *from the side,*
accompanied by the SENTRY.

Here is a dark sign from the gods –
what to make of this? I know her,
how can I deny it? That young girl's Antigone!
Wretched, child of a wretched father,
Oedipus. Look, is it possible?
They bring you in like a prisoner –
why? did you break the king's laws?
Did they take you in some act of mad defiance?

SENTRY:
She's the one, she did it single-handed –
we caught her burying the body. Where's Creon?

Enter CREON *from the palace.*

LEADER:
Back again, just in time when you need him.

CREON:
In time for what? What is it?

18

SENTRY: My king,
there's nothing you can swear you'll never do –
second thoughts make liars of us all.
I could have sworn I wouldn't hurry back
(what with your threats, the buffeting I just took),
but a stroke of luck beyond our wildest hopes,
what a joy, there's nothing like it. So,
back I've come, breaking my oath, who cares?
I'm bringing in our prisoner – this young girl –
we took her giving the dead the last rites.
But no casting lots this time; this is *my* luck,
my prize, no one else's.
                    Now, my lord,
here she is. Take her, question her,
cross-examine her to your heart's content.
But set me free, it's only right –
I'm rid of this dreadful business once for all.

CREON:
Prisoner! Her? You took her – where, doing what?

SENTRY:
Burying the man. That's the whole story.

CREON: What?
You mean what you say, you're telling me the truth?

SENTRY:
She's the one. With my own eyes I saw her
bury the body, just what you've forbidden.
There. Is that plain and clear?

CREON:
What did you see? Did you catch her in the act?

SENTRY:
Here's what happened. We went back to our post,
those threats of yours breathing down our necks –
we brushed the corpse clean of the dust that covered it,
stripped it bare . . . it was slimy, going soft,

and we took to high ground, backs to the wind
so the stink of him couldn't hit us;
jostling, baiting each other to keep awake,
shouting back and forth – no napping on the job,
not this time. And so the hours dragged by
until the sun stood dead above our heads,
a huge white ball in the noon sky, beating,
blazing down, and then it happened –
suddenly, a whirlwind!
Twisting a great dust-storm up from the earth,
a black plague of the heavens, filling the plain,
ripping the leaves off every tree in sight,
choking the air and sky. We squinted hard
and took our whipping from the gods.

And after the storm passed – it seemed endless –
there, we saw the girl!
And she cried out a sharp, piercing cry,
like a bird come back to an empty nest,
peering into its bed, and all the babies gone . . .
Just so, when she sees the corpse bare
she bursts into a long, shattering wail
and calls down withering curses on the heads
of all who did the work. And she scoops up dry dust,
handfuls, quickly, and lifting a fine bronze urn,
lifting it high and pouring, she crowns the dead
with three full libations.

                        Soon as we saw
we rushed her, closed on the kill like hunters,
and she, she didn't flinch. We interrogated her,
charging her with offenses past and present –
she stood up to it all, denied nothing. I tell you,
it made me ache and laugh in the same breath.
It's pure joy to escape the worst yourself,
it hurts a man to bring down his friends.
But all that, I'm afraid, means less to me
than my own skin. That's the way I'm made.

CREON: *Wheeling on* ANTIGONE.

                                        You,
with your eyes fixed on the ground – speak up.
Do you deny you did this, yes or no?

ANTIGONE:
I did it. I don't deny a thing.

CREON: *To the* SENTRY.
You, get out, wherever you please –
you're clear of a very heavy charge.

                          He leaves; CREON *turns back to*
                          ANTIGONE.

You, tell me briefly, no long speeches –
were you aware a decree had forbidden this?

ANTIGONE:
Well aware. How could I avoid it? It was public.

CREON:
And still you had the gall to break this law?

ANTIGONE:
Of course I did. It wasn't Zeus, not in the least,
who made this proclamation – not to me.
Nor did that Justice, dwelling with the gods
beneath the earth, ordain such laws for men.
Nor did I think your edict had such force
that you, a mere mortal, could override the gods,
the great unwritten, unshakable traditions.
They are alive, not just today or yesterday:
they live forever, from the first of time,
and no one knows when they first saw the light.

These laws – I was not about to break them,
not out of fear of some man's wounded pride,
and face the retribution of the gods.
Die I must, I've known it all my life –

how could I keep from knowing? – even without
your death-sentence ringing in my ears.
And if I am to die before my time
I consider that a gain. Who on earth,
alive in the midst of so much grief as I,
could fail to find his death a rich reward?
So for me, at least, to meet this doom of yours
is precious little pain. But if I had allowed
my own mother's son to rot, an unburied corpse –
that would have been an agony! This is nothing.
And if my present actions strike you as foolish,
let's just say I've been accused of folly
by a fool.

LEADER: Like father like daughter,
passionate, wild . . .
she hasn't learned to bend before adversity.

CREON:

No? Believe me, the stiffest stubborn wills
fall the hardest; the toughest iron,
tempered strong in the white-hot fire,
you'll see it crack and shatter first of all.
And I've known spirited horses you can break
with a light bit – proud, rebellious horses.
There's no room for pride, not in a slave,
not with the lord and master standing by.

This girl was an old hand at insolence
when she overrode the edicts we made public.
But once she had done it – the insolence,
twice over – to glory in it, laughing,
mocking us to our face with what she'd done.
I am not the man, not now: she is the man
if this victory goes to her and she goes free.

Never! Sister's child or closer in blood
than all my family clustered at my altar
worshiping Guardian Zeus – she'll never escape,

she and her blood sister, the most barbaric death.
Yes, I accuse her sister of an equal part
in scheming this, this burial.

To his attendants.

Bring her here!
I just saw her inside, hysterical, gone to pieces.
It never fails: the mind convicts itself
in advance, when scoundrels are up to no good,
plotting in the dark. Oh but I hate it more
when a traitor, caught red-handed,
tries to glorify his crimes.

ANTIGONE:
Creon, what more do you want
than my arrest and execution?

CREON:
Nothing. Then I have it all.

ANTIGONE:
Then why delay? Your moralizing repels me,
every word you say – pray god it always will.
So naturally all I say repels you too.
Enough.
Give me glory! What greater glory could I win
than to give my own brother decent burial?
These citizens here would all agree,

To the CHORUS.

they would praise me too
if their lips weren't locked in fear.

Pointing to CREON.

Lucky tyrants – the perquisites of power!
Ruthless power to do and say whatever pleases *them*.

CREON:
You alone, of all the people in Thebes,
see things that way.

ANTIGONE: They see it just that way
but defer to you and keep their tongues in leash.

CREON:
And you, aren't you ashamed to differ so from them?
So disloyal!

ANTIGONE: Not ashamed for a moment,
not to honor my brother, my own flesh and blood.

CREON:
Wasn't Eteocles a brother too – cut down, facing him?

ANTIGONE:
Brother, yes, by the same mother, the same father.

CREON:
Then how can you render his enemy such honors,
such impieties in his eyes?

ANTIGONE:
He will never testify to that,
Eteocles dead and buried.

CREON: He will –
if you honor the traitor just as much as him.

ANTIGONE:
But it was his brother, not some slave that died –

CREON:
Ravaging our country! –
but Eteocles died fighting in our behalf.

ANTIGONE:
No matter – Death longs for the same rites for all.

CREON:
Never the same for the patriot and the traitor.

ANTIGONE:
Who, Creon, who on earth can say the ones below
don't find this pure and uncorrupt?

CREON:
Never. Once an enemy, never a friend,
not even after death.

ANTIGONE:
I was born to join in love, not hate –
that is my nature.

CREON: Go down below and love,
if love you must – love the dead! While I'm alive,
no woman is going to lord it over me.

> *Enter* ISMENE *from the palace,*
> *under guard.*

CHORUS: Look,

Ismene's coming, weeping a sister's tears,
loving sister, under a cloud . . .
her face is flushed, her cheeks streaming.
Sorrow puts her lovely radiance in the dark.

CREON: You –
in my own house, you viper, slinking undetected,
sucking my life-blood! I never knew
I was breeding twin disasters, the two of you
rising up against my throne. Come, tell me,
will you confess your part in the crime or not?
Answer me. Swear to me.

ISMENE: I did it, yes –
if only she consents – I share the guilt,
the consequences too.

ANTIGONE: No,
Justice will never suffer that – not you,
you were unwilling. I never brought you in.

ISMENE:
But now you face such dangers . . . I'm not ashamed
to sail through trouble with you,
make your troubles mine.

ANTIGONE: Who did the work?
Let the dead and the god of death bear witness!
I have no love for a friend who loves in words alone.

ISMENE:
Oh no, my sister, don't reject me, please,
let me die beside you, consecrating
the dead together.

ANTIGONE: Never share my dying,
don't lay claim to what you never touched.
My death will be enough.

ISMENE:
What do I care for life, cut off from you?

ANTIGONE:
Ask Creon. Your concern is all for him.

ISMENE:
Why abuse me so? It doesn't help you now.

ANTIGONE: You're right –
if I mock you, I get no pleasure from it,
only pain.

ISMENE: Tell me, dear one,
what can I do to help you, even now?

ANTIGONE:
Save yourself. I don't grudge you your survival.

ISMENE:
Oh no, no, denied my portion in your death?

ANTIGONE:
You chose to live, I chose to die.

ISMENE: Not, at least,
without every kind of caution I could voice.

ANTIGONE:
Your wisdom appealed to one world – mine, another.

ISMENE:
But look, we're both guilty, both condemned to death.

ANTIGONE:
Courage! Live your life. I gave myself to death,
long ago, so I might serve the dead.

CREON:
They're both mad, I tell you, the two of them.
One's just shown it, the other's been that way
since she was born.

ISMENE: True, my king,
the sense we were born with cannot last forever . . .
commit cruelty on a person long enough
and the mind begins to go.

CREON: Yours did,
when you chose to commit your crimes with her.

ISMENE:
How can I live alone, without her?

CREON: Her?
Don't even mention her – she no longer exists.

ISMENE:
What? You'd kill your own son's bride?

CREON: Absolutely:
there are other fields for him to plow.

ISMENE: Perhaps,
but never as true, as close a bond as theirs.

CREON:
A worthless woman for my son? It repels me.

Sophocles

ISMENE:
Dearest Haemon, your father wrongs you so!

CREON:
Enough, enough – you and your talk of marriage!

ISMENE:
Creon – you're really going to rob your son of Antigone?

CREON:
Death will do it for me – break their marriage off.

LEADER:
So, it's settled then? Antigone must die?

CREON:
Settled, yes – we both know that.

To the guards.

Stop wasting time. Take them in.
From now on they'll act like women.
Tie them up, no more running loose;
even the bravest will cut and run,
once they see Death coming for their lives.

The guards escort ANTIGONE *and*
ISMENE *into the palace.* CREON
remains while the old citizens form
their CHORUS.

CHORUS:
Blest, they are the truly blest who all their lives
have never tasted devastation. For others, once
the gods have rocked a house to its foundations
   the ruin will never cease, cresting on and on
from one generation on throughout the race –
like a great mounting tide
driven on by savage northern gales,
   surging over the dead black depths
roiling up from the bottom dark heaves of sand

28

and the headlands, taking the storm's onslaught full-force,
roar, and the low moaning

             echoes on and on

                    and now

as in ancient times I see the sorrows of the house,
the living heirs of the old ancestral kings,
piling on the sorrows of the dead

  and one generation cannot free the next –
some god will bring them crashing down,
the race finds no release.
And now the light, the hope

    springing up from the late last root
in the house of Oedipus, that hope's cut down in turn
by the long, bloody knife swung by the gods of death
by a senseless word

            by fury at the heart.

                       Zeus,

yours is the power, Zeus, what man on earth
can override it, who can hold it back?
Power that neither Sleep, the all-ensnaring

  no, nor the tireless months of heaven
can ever overmaster – young through all time,
mighty lord of power, you hold fast

  the dazzling crystal mansions of Olympus.
And throughout the future, late and soon
as through the past, your law prevails:
no towering form of greatness

  enters into the lives of mortals

                free and clear of ruin.

                       True,

our dreams, our high hopes voyaging far and wide
bring sheer delight to many, to many others

  delusion, blithe, mindless lusts
and the fraud steals on one slowly . . . unaware
till he trips and puts his foot into the fire.

  He was a wise old man who coined
the famous saying: 'Sooner or later

foul is fair, fair is foul
to the man the gods will ruin' –
    He goes his way for a moment only
                    free of blinding ruin.

                        Enter HAEMON *from the palace.*

    Here's Haemon now, the last of all your sons.
    Does he come in tears for his bride,
    his doomed bride, Antigone –
    bitter at being cheated of their marriage?

CREON:
We'll soon know, better than seers could tell us.

                        Turning to HAEMON.

Son, you've heard the final verdict on your bride?
Are you coming now, raving against your father?
Or do you love me, no matter what I do?

HAEMON:
Father, I'm your *son* . . . you in your wisdom
set my bearings for me – I obey you.
No marriage could ever mean more to me than you,
whatever good direction you may offer.

CREON: Fine, Haemon.
That's how you ought to feel within your heart,
subordinate to your father's will in every way.
That's what a man prays for: to produce good sons –
a household full of them, dutiful and attentive,
so they can pay his enemy back with interest
and match the respect their father shows his friend.
But the man who rears a brood of useless children,
what has he brought into the world, I ask you?
Nothing but trouble for himself, and mockery
from his enemies laughing in his face.

                        Oh Haemon,
never lose your sense of judgment over a woman.

The warmth, the rush of pleasure, it all goes cold
in your arms, I warn you . . . a worthless woman
in your house, a misery in your bed.
What wound cuts deeper than a loved one
turned against you? Spit her out,
like a mortal enemy – let the girl go.
Let her find a husband down among the dead.
Imagine it: I caught her in naked rebellion,
the traitor, the only one in the whole city.
I'm not about to prove myself a liar,
not to my people, no, I'm going to kill her!
That's right – so let her cry for mercy, sing her hymns
to Zeus who defends all bonds of kindred blood.
Why, if I bring up my own kin to be rebels,
think what I'd suffer from the world at large.
Show me the man who rules his household well:
I'll show you someone fit to rule the state.
That good man, my son,
I have every confidence he and he alone
can give commands and take them too. Staunch
in the storm of spears he'll stand his ground,
a loyal, unflinching comrade at your side.

But whoever steps out of line, violates the laws
or presumes to hand out orders to his superiors,
he'll win no praise from me. But that man
the city places in authority, his orders
must be obeyed, large and small,
right and wrong.
          Anarchy –
show me a greater crime in all the earth!
She, she destroys cities, rips up houses,
breaks the ranks of spearmen into headlong rout.
But the ones who last it out, the great mass of them
owe their lives to discipline. Therefore
we must defend the men who live by law,
never let some woman triumph over us.
Better to fall from power, if fall we must,

31

at the hands of a man – never be rated
inferior to a woman, never.

LEADER: To us,
unless old age has robbed us of our wits,
you seem to say what you have to say with sense.

HAEMON:
Father, only the gods endow a man with reason,
the finest of all their gifts, a treasure.
Far be it from me – I haven't the skill,
and certainly no desire, to tell you when,
if ever, you make a slip in speech . . . though
someone else might have a good suggestion.

Of course it's not for you,
in the normal run of things, to watch
whatever men say or do, or find to criticize.
The man in the street, you know, dreads your glance,
he'd never say anything displeasing to your face.
But it's for me to catch the murmurs in the dark,
the way the city mourns for this young girl.
'No woman,' they say, 'ever deserved death less,
and such a brutal death for such a glorious action.
She, with her own dear brother lying in his blood –
she couldn't bear to leave him dead, unburied,
food for the wild dogs or wheeling vultures.
Death? She deserves a glowing crown of gold!'
So they say, and the rumor spreads in secret,
darkly . . .

                I rejoice in your success, father –
nothing more precious to me in the world.
What medal of honor brighter to his children
than a father's growing glory? Or a child's
to his proud father? Now don't, please,
be quite so single-minded, self-involved,
or assume the world is wrong and you are right.
Whoever thinks that he alone possesses intelligence,

the gift of eloquence, he and no one else,
and character too . . . such men, I tell you,
spread them open – you will find them empty.

                                                No,

it's no disgrace for a man, even a wise man,
to learn many things and not to be too rigid.
You've seen trees by a raging winter torrent,
how many sway with the flood and salvage every twig,
but not the stubborn – they're ripped out, roots and all.
Bend or break. The same when a man is sailing:
haul your sheets too taut, never give an inch,
you'll capsize, and go the rest of the voyage
keel up and the rowing-benches under.

Oh give way. Relax your anger – change!
I'm young, I know, but let me offer this:
it would be best by far, I admit,
if a man were born infallible, right by nature.
If not – and things don't often go that way,
it's best to learn from those with good advice.

LEADER:
You'd do well, my lord, if he's speaking to the point,
to learn from him,

                         Turning to HAEMON.

                  and you, my boy, from him.
You both are talking sense.

CREON: So,
men our age, we're to be lectured, are we? –
schooled by a boy his age?

HAEMON:
Only in what is right. But if I seem young,
look less to my years and more to what I do.

CREON:
Do? Is admiring rebels an achievement?

HAEMON:
I'd never suggest that you admire treason.

CREON: Oh? –
isn't that just the sickness that's attacked her?

HAEMON:
The whole city of Thebes denies it, to a man.

CREON:
And is Thebes about to tell me how to rule?

HAEMON:
Now, you see? Who's talking like a child?

CREON:
Am I to rule this land for others – or myself?

HAEMON:
It's no city at all, owned by one man alone.

CREON:
What? The city *is* the king's – that's the law!

HAEMON:
What a splendid king you'd make of a desert island –
you and you alone.

CREON: *To the* CHORUS.
                    This boy, I do believe,
is fighting on her side, the woman's side.

HAEMON:
If you are a woman, yes –
my concern is all for you.

CREON:
Why, you degenerate – bandying accusations,
threatening me with justice, your own father!

HAEMON:
I see my father offending justice – wrong.

CREON: Wrong?
To protect my royal rights?

HAEMON: Protect your rights?
When you trample down the honors of the gods?

CREON:
You, you soul of corruption, rotten through –
woman's accomplice!

HAEMON: That may be,
but you will never find me accomplice to a criminal.

CREON:
That's what *she* is,
and every word you say is a blatant appeal for her –

HAEMON:
And you, and me, and the gods beneath the earth.

CREON:
You will never marry her, not while she's alive.

HAEMON:
Then she will die . . . but her death will kill another.

CREON:
What, brazen threats? You go too far!

HAEMON: What threat?
Combating your empty, mindless judgments with a word?

CREON:
You'll suffer for your sermons, you and your empty wisdom!

HAEMON:
If you weren't my father, I'd say you were insane.

CREON:
Don't flatter me with Father – you woman's slave!

HAEMON:
You really expect to fling abuse at me

and not receive the same?

CREON: Is that so!
Now, by heaven, I promise you, you'll pay –
taunting, insulting me! Bring her out,
that hateful – she'll die now, here,
in front of his eyes, beside her groom!

HAEMON:
No, no, she will never die beside me –
don't delude yourself. And you will never
see me, never set eyes on my face again.
Rage your heart out, rage with friends
who can stand the sight of you.

> *Rushing out.*

LEADER:
Gone, my king, in a burst of anger.
A temper young as his . . . hurt him once,
he may do something violent.

CREON: Let him do –
dream up something desperate, past all human limit!
Good riddance. Rest assured,
he'll never save those two young girls from death.

LEADER:
Both of them, you really intend to kill them both?

CREON:
No, not her, the one whose hands are clean –
you're quite right.

LEADER: But Antigone –
what sort of death do you have in mind for her?

CREON:
I will take her down some wild, desolate path
never trod by men, and wall her up alive
in a rocky vault, and set out short rations,
just the measure piety demands

to keep the entire city free of defilement.
There let her pray to the one god she worships:
Death – who knows? – may just reprieve her from death.
Or she may learn at last, better late than never,
what a waste of breath it is to worship Death.

Exit to the palace.

CHORUS:
Love, never conquered in battle
Love the plunderer laying waste the rich!
Love standing the night-watch
                    guarding a girl's soft cheek,
you range the seas, the shepherds' steadings off in the wilds –
not even the deathless gods can flee your onset,
nothing human born for a day –
whoever feels your grip is driven mad.
                            Love! –
you wrench the minds of the righteous into outrage,
swerve them to their ruin – you have ignited this,
this kindred strife, father and son at war
                    and Love alone the victor –
warm glance of the bride triumphant, burning with desire!
Throned in power, side-by-side with the mighty laws!
Irresistible Aphrodite, never conquered –
Love, you mock us for your sport.

ANTIGONE *is brought from the*
palace under guard.

But now, even I would rebel against the king,
I would break all bounds when I see this –
I fill with tears, I cannot hold them back,
not any more . . . I see Antigone make her way
to the bridal vault where all are laid to rest.

ANTIGONE:
Look at me, men of my fatherland,
    setting out on the last road

looking into the last light of day
the last I will ever see . . .
the god of death who puts us all to bed
takes me down to the banks of Acheron alive –
   denied my part in the wedding-songs,
no wedding-song in the dusk has crowned my marriage –
I go to wed the lord of the dark waters.

CHORUS:

   Not crowned with glory or with a dirge,
   you leave for the deep pit of the dead.
   No withering illness laid you low,
   no strokes of the sword – a law to yourself,
   alone, no mortal like you, ever, you go down
   to the halls of Death alive and breathing.

ANTIGONE:

But think of Niobe – well I know her story –
   think what a living death she died,
Tantalus' daughter, stranger queen from the east:
there on the mountain heights, growing stone
binding as ivy, slowly walled her round
and the rains will never cease, the legends say
the snows will never leave her . . .
   wasting away, under her brows the tears
showering down her breasting ridge and slopes –
a rocky death like hers puts me to sleep.

CHORUS:

   But she was a god, born of gods,
   and we are only mortals born to die.
   And yet, of course, it's a great thing
   for a dying girl to hear, even to hear
   she shares a destiny equal to the gods,
   during life and later, once she's dead.

ANTIGONE: O you mock me!
Why, in the name of all my fathers' gods
why can't you wait till I am gone –

must you abuse me to my face?
O my city, all your fine rich sons!
And you, you springs of the Dirce,
holy grove of Thebes where the chariots gather,
    you at least, you'll bear me witness, look,
unmourned by friends and forced by such crude laws
I go to my rockbound prison, strange new tomb –
    always a stranger, O dear god,
    I have no home on earth and none below,
      not with the living, not with the breathless dead.

CHORUS:
    You went too far, the last limits of daring –
    smashing against the high throne of Justice!
      Your life's in ruins, child – I wonder . . .
    do you pay for your father's terrible ordeal?

ANTIGONE:
There – at last you've touched it, the worst pain
the worst anguish! Raking up the grief for father
    three times over, for all the doom
that's struck us down, the brilliant house of Laius.
O mother, your marriage-bed
the coiling horrors, the coupling there –
    you with your own son, my father – doomstruck mother!
Such, such were my parents, and I their wretched child.
I go to them now, cursed, unwed, to share their home –
    I am a stranger! O dear brother, doomed
    in your marriage – your marriage murders mine,
    your dying drags me down to death alive!

                    Enter Creon.

CHORUS:
    Reverence asks some reverence in return –
    but attacks on power never go unchecked,
      not by the man who holds the reins of power.
    Your own blind will, your passion has destroyed you.

39

ANTIGONE:

No one to weep for me, my friends,
no wedding-song – they take me away
in all my pain . . . the road lies open, waiting.
Never again, the law forbids me to see
the sacred eye of day. I am agony!
No tears for the destiny that's mine,
no loved one mourns my death.

CREON: Can't you see?
If a man could wail his own dirge *before* he dies,
he'd never finish.

                                        To the guards.

                    Take her away, quickly!
Wall her up in the tomb, you have your orders.
Abandon her there, alone, and let her choose –
death or a buried life with a good roof for shelter.
As for myself, my hands are clean. This young girl –
dead or alive, she will be stripped of her rights,
her stranger's rights, here in the world above.

ANTIGONE:

O tomb, my bridal-bed – my house, my prison
cut in the hollow rock, my everlasting watch!
I'll soon be there, soon embrace my own,
the great growing family of our dead
Persephone has received among her ghosts.

                                                        I,

the last of them all, the most reviled by far,
go down before my destined time's run out.
But still I go, cherishing one good hope:
my arrival may be dear to father,
dear to you, my mother,
dear to you, my loving brother, Eteocles –
When you died I washed you with my hands,
I dressed you all, I poured the sacred cups
across your tombs. But now, Polynices,

because I laid your body out as well,
this, this is my reward. Nevertheless
I honored you – the decent will admit it –
well and wisely too.
                         Never, I tell you,
if I had been the mother of children
or if my husband died, exposed and rotting –
I'd never have taken this ordeal upon myself,
never defied our people's will. What law,
you ask, do I satisfy with what I say?
A husband dead, there might have been another.
A child by another too, if I had lost the first.
But mother and father both lost in the halls of Death,
no brother could ever spring to light again.
For this law alone I held you first in honor.
For this, Creon, the king, judges me a criminal
guilty of dreadful outrage, my dear brother!
And now he leads me off, a captive in his hands,
with no part in the bridal-song, the bridal-bed,
denied all joy of marriage, raising children –
deserted so by loved ones, struck by fate,
I descend alive to the caverns of the dead.

What law of the mighty gods have I transgressed?
Why look to the heavens any more, tormented as I am?
Whom to call, what comrades now? Just think,
my reverence only brands me for irreverence!
Very well: if this is the pleasure of the gods,
once I suffer I will know that I was wrong.
But if these men are wrong, let them suffer
nothing worse than they mete out to me –
these masters of injustice!

LEADER:
Still the same rough winds, the wild passion
raging through the girl.

CREON: *To the guards.*
                              Take her away.
You're wasting time – you'll pay for it too.

ANTIGONE:
Oh god, the voice of death. It's come, it's here.

CREON:
True. Not a word of hope – your doom is sealed.

ANTIGONE:
　　Land of Thebes, city of all my fathers –
　　O you gods, the first gods of the race!
　　They drag me away, now, no more delay.
　　Look on me, you noble sons of Thebes –
　　the last of a great line of kings,
　　I alone, see what I suffer now
　　at the hands of what breed of men –
　　all for reverence, my reverence for the gods!

> *She leaves under guard: the* CHORUS
> *gathers.*

CHORUS:
　　Danaë, Danaë –
even she endured a fate like yours,
　　in all her lovely strength she traded
the light of day for the bolted brazen vault –
buried within her tomb, her bridal-chamber,
wed to the yoke and broken.
　　But she was of glorious birth
　　　　　　　　my child, my child
and treasured the seed of Zeus within her womb,
the cloudburst streaming gold!
　　The power of fate is a wonder,
　　dark, terrible wonder –
　　neither wealth nor armies
　　towered walls nor ships
　　black hulls lashed by the salt
　　can save us from that force.

The yoke tamed him too
   young Lycurgus flaming in anger
king of Edonia, all for his mad taunts
Dionysus clamped him down, encased
in the chain-mail of rock
   and there his rage
          his terrible flowering rage burst –
sobbing, dying away . . . at last that madman
came to know his god –
      the power he mocked, the power
      he taunted in all his frenzy
      trying to stamp out
      the women strong with the god –
      the torch, the raving sacred cries –
      enraging the Muses who adore the flute.
And far north where the Black Rocks
   cut the sea in half
and murderous straits
split the coast of Thrace
 a forbidding city stands
where once, hard by the walls
the savage Ares thrilled to watch
a king's new queen, a Fury rearing in rage
 against his two royal sons –
   her bloody hands, her dagger-shuttle
stabbing out their eyes – cursed, blinding wounds –
their eyes blind sockets screaming for revenge!

They wailed in agony, cries echoing cries
   the princes doomed at birth . . .
and their mother doomed to chains,
walled up in a tomb of stone –
 but she traced her own birth back
to a proud Athenian line and the high gods
and off in caverns half the world away,
born of the wild North Wind
 she sprang on her father's gales,

racing stallions up the leaping cliffs –
child of the heavens. But even on her the Fates
the gray everlasting Fates rode hard
my child, my child.

> *Enter* TIRESIAS, *the blind prophet,*
> *led by a boy.*

TIRESIAS: Lords of Thebes,
I and the boy have come together,
hand in hand. Two see with the eyes of one . . .
so the blind must go, with a guide to lead the way.

CREON:
What is it, old Tiresias? What news now?

TIRESIAS:
I will teach you. And you obey the seer.

CREON: I will,
I've never wavered from your advice before.

TIRESIAS:
And so you kept the city straight on course.

CREON:
I owe you a great deal, I swear to that.

TIRESIAS:
Then reflect, my son: you are poised,
once more, on the razor-edge of fate.

CREON:
What is it? I shudder to hear you.

TIRESIAS: You will learn
when you listen to the warnings of my craft.
As I sat on the ancient seat of augury,
in the sanctuary where every bird I know
will hover at my hands – suddenly I heard it,
a strange voice in the wingbeats, unintelligible,

barbaric, a mad scream! Talons flashing, ripping,
they were killing each other – that much I knew –
the murderous fury whirring in those wings
made that much clear!
                                    I was afraid,
I turned quickly, tested the burnt-sacrifice,
ignited the altar at all points – but no fire,
the god in the fire never blazed.
Not from those offerings . . . over the embers
slid a heavy ooze from the long thighbones,
smoking, sputtering out, and the bladder
puffed and burst – spraying gall into the air –
and the fat wrapping the bones slithered off
and left them glistening white. No fire!
The rites failed that might have blazed the future
with a sign. So I learned from the boy here:
he is my guide, as I am guide to others.
                                    And it is you –
your high resolve that sets this plague on Thebes.
The public altars and sacred hearths are fouled,
one and all, by the birds and dogs with carrion
torn from the corpse, the doomstruck son of Oedipus!
And so the gods are deaf to our prayers, they spurn
the offerings in our hands, the flame of holy flesh.
No birds cry out an omen clear and true –
they're gorged with the murdered victim's blood and fat.
Take these things to heart, my son, I warn you.
All men make mistakes, it is only human.
But once the wrong is done, a man
can turn his back on folly, misfortune too,
if he tries to make amends, however low he's fallen,
and stops his bullnecked ways. Stubbornness
brands you for stupidity – pride is a crime.
No, yield to the dead!
Never stab the fighter when he's down.
Where's the glory, killing the dead twice over?

I mean you well. I give you sound advice.
It's best to learn from a good adviser
when he speaks for your own good:
it's pure gain.

CREON: Old man – all of you! So,
you shoot your arrows at my head like archers at the target –
I even have *him* loosed on me, this fortune-teller.
Oh his ilk has tried to sell me short
and ship me off for years. Well,
drive your bargains, traffic – much as you like –
in the gold of India, silver-gold of Sardis.
You'll never bury that body in the grave,
not even if Zeus's eagles rip the corpse
and wing their rotten pickings off to the throne of god!
Never, not even in fear of such defilement
will I tolerate his burial, that traitor.
Well I know, we can't defile the gods –
no mortal has the power.
                         No,
reverend old Tiresias, all men fall,
it's only human, but the wisest fall obscenely
when they glorify obscene advice with rhetoric –
all for their own gain.

TIRESIAS:
Oh god, is there a man alive
who knows, who actually believes . . .

CREON: What now?
What earth-shattering truth are you about to utter?

TIRESIAS:
. . . just how much a sense of judgment, wisdom
is the greatest gift we have?

CREON: Just as much, I'd say,
as a twisted mind is the worst affliction known.

TIRESIAS:
You are the one who's sick, Creon, sick to death.

CREON:
I am in no mood to trade insults with a seer.

TIRESIAS:
You have already, calling my prophecies a lie.

CREON: Why not?
You and the whole breed of seers are mad for money!

TIRESIAS:
And the whole race of tyrants lusts for filthy gain.

CREON:
This slander of yours –
are you aware you're speaking to the king?

TIRESIAS:
Well aware. Who helped you save the city?

CREON: You –
you have your skills, old seer, but you lust for injustice!

TIRESIAS:
You will drive me to utter the dreadful secret in my heart.

CREON:
Spit it out! Just don't speak it out for profit.

TIRESIAS:
Profit? No, not a bit of profit, not for you.

CREON:
Know full well, you'll never buy off my resolve.

TIRESIAS:
Then know this too, learn this by heart!
The chariot of the sun will not race through
so many circuits more, before you have surrendered
one born of your own loins, your own flesh and blood,
a corpse for corpses given in return, since you have thrust

to the world below a child sprung for the world above,
ruthlessly lodged a living soul within the grave –
then you've robbed the gods below the earth,
keeping a dead body here in the bright air,
unburied, unsung, unhallowed by the rites.

You, you have no business with the dead,
nor do the gods above – this is violence
you have forced upon the heavens.
And so the avengers, the dark destroyers late
but true to the mark, now lie in wait for you,
the Furies sent by the gods and the god of death
to strike you down with the pains that you perfected!

There. Reflect on that, tell me I've been bribed.
The day comes soon, no long test of time, not now,
when the mourning cries for men and women break
throughout your halls. Great hatred rises against you –
cities in tumult, all whose mutilated sons
the dogs have graced with burial, or the wild beasts
or a wheeling crow that wings the ungodly stench of carrion
back to each city, each warrior's hearth and home.

These arrows for your heart! Since you've raked me
I loose them like an archer in my anger,
arrows deadly true. You'll never escape
their burning, searing force.

Motioning to his escort.

Come, boy, take me home.
So he can vent his rage on younger men,
and learn to keep a gentler tongue in his head
and better sense than what he carries now.

Exit to the side.

LEADER:
The old man's gone, my king –
terrible prophecies. Well I know,

since the hair on this old head went gray,
he's never lied to Thebes.

CREON:

I know it myself – I'm shaken, torn.
It's a dreadful thing to yield . . . but resist now?
Lay my pride bare to the blows of ruin?
That's dreadful too.

LEADER: But good advice,
Creon, take it now, you must.

CREON:

What should I do? Tell me . . . I'll obey.

LEADER:

Go! Free the girl from the rocky vault
and raise a mound for the body you exposed.

CREON:

That's your advice? You think I should give in?

LEADER:

Yes, my king, quickly. Disasters sent by the gods
cut short our follies in a flash.

CREON: Oh it's hard,
giving up the heart's desire . . . but I will do it –
no more fighting a losing battle with necessity.

LEADER:

Do it now, go, don't leave it to others.

CREON:

Now – I'm on my way! Come, each of you,
take up axes, make for the high ground,
over there, quickly! I and my better judgment
have come round to this – I shackled her,
I'll set her free myself. I am afraid . . .
it's best to keep the established laws
to the very day we die.

*Rushing out, followed by his
entourage. The* CHORUS *clusters
around the altar.*

CHORUS:
God of a hundred names!
      Great Dionysus –
   Son and glory of Semele! Pride of Thebes –
Child of Zeus whose thunder rocks the clouds –
Lord of the famous lands of evening –
King of the Mysteries!
        King of Eleusis, Demeter's plain
her breasting hills that welcome in the world –
Great Dionysus!
       Bacchus, living in Thebes
the mother-city of all your frenzied women –
           Bacchus
  living along the Ismenus' rippling waters
standing over the field sown with the Dragon's teeth!

You – we have seen you through the flaring smoky fires,
 your torches blazing over the twin peaks
where nymphs of the hallowed cave climb onward
      fired with you, your sacred rage –
we have seen you at Castalia's running spring
and down from the heights of Nysa crowned with ivy
the greening shore rioting vines and grapes
 down you come in your storm of wild women
      ecstatic, mystic cries –
         Dionysus –
down to watch and ward the roads of Thebes!
First of all cities, Thebes you honor first
you and your mother, bride of the lighting –
come, Dionysus! now your people lie
in the iron grip of plague,
come in your racing, healing stride
      down Parnassus' slopes
or across the moaning straits.

                    Lord of the dancing –
dance, dance the constellations breathing fire!
Great master of the voices of the night!
Child of Zeus, God's offspring, come, come forth!
Lord, king, dance with your nymphs, swirling, raving
arm-in-arm in frenzy through the night
 they dance you, Iacchus –
                    Dance, Dionysus
giver of all good things!

                              Enter a MESSENGER *from the side.*

MESSENGER: Neighbors,
friends of the house of Cadmus and the kings,
there's not a thing in this mortal life of ours
I'd praise or blame as settled once for all.
Fortune lifts and Fortune fells the lucky
and unlucky every day. No prophet on earth
can tell a man his fate. Take Creon:
there was a man to rouse your envy once,
as I see it. He saved the realm from enemies,
taking power, he alone, the lord of the fatherland,
he set us true on course – he flourished like a tree
with the noble line of sons he bred and reared . . .
and now it's lost, all gone.
                              Believe me,
when a man has squandered his true joys,
he's good as dead, I tell you, a living corpse.
Pile up riches in your house, as much as you like –
live like a king with a huge show of pomp,
but if real delight is missing from the lot,
I wouldn't give you a wisp of smoke for it,
not compared with joy.

LEADER: What now?
What new grief do you bring the house of kings?

MESSENGER:
Dead, dead – and the living are guilty of their death!

LEADER:
Who's the murderer? Who is dead? Tell us.

MESSENGER:
Haemon's gone, his blood spilled by the very hand –

LEADER:
His father's or his own?

MESSENGER: His own . . .
raging mad with his father for the death –

LEADER: Oh great seer,
you saw it all, you brought your word to birth!

MESSENGER:
Those are the facts. Deal with them as you will.

> *As he turns to go,* EURYDICE *enters
> from the palace.*

LEADER:
Look, Eurydice. Poor woman, Creon's wife,
so close at hand. By chance perhaps,
unless she's heard the news about her son.

EURYDICE: My countrymen,
all of you – I caught the sound of your words
as I was leaving to do my part,
to appeal to queen Athena with my prayers.
I was just loosing the bolts, opening the doors,
when a voice filled with sorrow, family sorrow,
struck my ears, and I fell back, terrified,
into the women's arms – everything went black.
Tell me the news, again, whatever it is . . .
sorrow and I are hardly strangers.
I can bear the worst.

MESSENGER: I – dear lady,
I'll speak as an eye-witness. I was there.
And I won't pass over one word of the truth.
Why should I try to soothe you with a story,

only to prove a liar in a moment?
Truth is always best.
          So,
I escorted your lord, I guided him
to the edge of the plain where the body lay,
Polynices, torn by the dogs and still unmourned.
And saying a prayer to Hecate of the Crossroads,
Pluto too, to hold their anger and be kind,
we washed the dead in a bath of holy water
and plucking some fresh branches, gathering . . .
what was left of him, we burned them all together
and raised a high mound of native earth, and then
we turned and made for that rocky vault of hers,
the hollow, empty bed of the bride of Death.
And far off, one of us heard a voice,
a long wail rising, echoing
out of that unhallowed wedding-chamber,
he ran to alert the master and Creon pressed on,
closer – the strange, inscrutable cry came sharper,
throbbing around him now, and he let loose
a cry of his own, enough to wrench the heart,
'Oh god, am I the prophet now? going down
the darkest road I've ever gone? My son –
it's *his* dear voice, he greets me! Go, men,
closer, quickly! Go through the gap,
the rocks are dragged back –
right to the tomb's very mouth – and look,
see if it's Haemon's voice I think I hear,
or the gods have robbed me of my senses.'

The king was shattered. We took his orders,
went and searched, and there in the deepest,
dark recesses of the tomb we found her . . .
hanged by the neck in a fine linen noose,
strangled in her veils – and the boy,
his arms flung around her waist,
clinging to her, wailing for his bride,

dead and down below, for his father's crimes
and the bed of his marriage blighted by misfortune.
When Creon saw him, he gave a deep sob,
he ran in, shouting, crying out to him,
'Oh my child – what have you done? what seized you,
what insanity? what disaster drove you mad?
Come out, my son! I beg you on my knees!'
But the boy gave him a wild burning glance,
spat in his face, not a word in reply,
he drew his sword – his father rushed out,
running as Haemon lunged and missed! –
and then, doomed, desperate with himself,
suddenly leaning his full weight on the blade,
he buried it in his body, halfway to the hilt,
And still in his senses, pouring his arms around her,
he embraced the girl and breathing hard,
released a quick rush of blood,
bright red on her cheek glistening white.
And there he lies, body enfolding body . . .
he has won his bride at last, poor boy,
not here but in the houses of the dead.

Creon shows the world that of all the ills
afflicting men the worst is lack of judgment.

EURYDICE *turns and re-enters the*
palace.

LEADER:
What do you make of that? The lady's gone,
without a word, good or bad.

MESSENGER: I'm alarmed too
but here's my hope – faced with her son's death
she finds it unbecoming to mourn in public.
Inside, under her roof, she'll set her women
to the task and wail the sorrow of the house.
She's too discreet. She won't do something rash.

LEADER:

I'm not so sure. To me, at least,
a long heavy silence promises danger,
just as much as a lot of empty outcries.

MESSENGER:

We'll see if she's holding something back,
hiding some passion in her heart.
I'm going in. You may be right – who knows?
Even too much silence has its dangers.

> *Exit to the palace. Enter* CREON
> *from the side, escorted by attendants*
> *carrying* HAEMON's *body on a bier.*

LEADER:

    The king himself! Coming toward us,
    look, holding the boy's head in his hands.
    Clear, damning proof, if it's right to say so –
    proof of his own madness, no one else's,
        no, his own blind wrongs.

CREON: Ohhh,
so senseless, so insane . . . my crimes,
my stubborn, deadly –
Look at us, the killer, the killed,
father and son, the same blood – the misery!
My plans, my mad fanatic heart,
my son, cut off so young!
Ai, dead, lost to the world,
not through your stupidity, no, my own.

LEADER: Too late,
too late, you see what justice means.

CREON: Oh I've learned
    through blood and tears! Then, it was then,
    when the god came down and struck me – a great weight
    shattering, driving me down that wild savage path,

ruining, trampling down my joy. Oh the agony,
the heartbreaking agonies of our lives.

> *Enter the* MESSENGER *from the palace.*

MESSENGER: Master,
what a hoard of grief you have, and you'll have more.
The grief that lies to hand you've brought yourself –

> *Pointing to* HAEMON's *body.*

the rest, in the house, you'll see it all too soon.

CREON:
What now? What's worse than this?

MESSENGER: The queen is dead.
The mother of this dead boy . . . mother to the end –
poor thing, her wounds are fresh.

CREON: No, no,
harbor of Death, so choked, so hard to cleanse! –
why me? why are you killing me?
Herald of pain, more words, more grief?
I died once, you kill me again and again!
What's the report, boy . . . some news for me?
My wife dead? O dear god!
Slaughter heaped on slaughter?

> *The doors open; the body of*
> EURYDICE *is brought out on her bier.*

MESSENGER: See for yourself:
now they bring her body from the palace.

CREON: Oh no,
another, a second loss to break the heart.
What next, what fate still waits for me?
I just held my son in my arms and now,
look, a new corpse rising before my eyes –
wretched, helpless mother – O my son!

MESSENGER:
She stabbed herself at the altar,
then her eyes went dark, after she'd raised
a cry for the noble fate of Megareus, the hero
killed in the first assault, then for Haemon,
then with her dying breath she called down
torments on your head – you killed her sons.

CREON: Oh the dread,
I shudder with dread! Why not kill me too? –
run me through with a good sharp sword?
Oh god, the misery, anguish –
I, I'm churning with it, going under.

MESSENGER:
Yes, and the dead, the woman lying there,
piles the guilt of all their deaths on you.

CREON:
How did she end her life, what bloody stroke?

MESSENGER:
She drove home to the heart with her own hand,
once she learned her son was dead . . . that agony.

CREON:
And the guilt is all mine –
can never be fixed on another man,
no escape for me. I killed you,
I, god help me, I admit it all!

                              To his attendants.

Take me away, quickly, out of sight.
I don't even exist – I'm no one. Nothing.

LEADER:
Good advice, if there's any good in suffering.
Quickest is best when troubles block the way.

57

CREON: *Kneeling in prayer.*
     Come, let it come! – that best of fates for me
     that brings the final day, best fate of all.
     Oh quickly, now –
     so I never have to see another sunrise.

LEADER:
That will come when it comes;
we must deal with all that lies before us.
The future rests with the ones who tend the future.

CREON:
That prayer – I poured my heart into that prayer!

LEADER:
No more prayers now. For mortal men
there is no escape from the doom we must endure.

CREON:
     Take me away, I beg you, out of sight.
     A rash, indiscriminate fool!
     I murdered you, my son, against my will –
     you too, my wife . . .
                              Wailing wreck of a man,
     whom to look to? where to lean for support?

                         Desperately turning from HAEMON
                         to EURYDICE *on their biers.*

     Whatever I touch goes wrong – once more
     a crushing fate's come down upon my head!

                         The MESSENGER *and attendants lead*
                         CREON *into the palace.*

CHORUS:
     Wisdom is by far the greatest part of joy,
     and reverence toward the gods must be safeguarded.
     The mighty words of the proud are paid in full
     with mighty blows of fate, and at long last
     those blows will teach us wisdom.

                         The old citizens exit to the side.

1. BOCCACCIO · *Mrs Rosie and the Priest*
2. GERARD MANLEY HOPKINS · *As kingfishers catch fire*
3. *The Saga of Gunnlaug Serpent-tongue*
4. THOMAS DE QUINCEY · *On Murder Considered as One of the Fine Arts*
5. FRIEDRICH NIETZSCHE · *Aphorisms on Love and Hate*
6. JOHN RUSKIN · *Traffic*
7. PU SONGLING · *Wailing Ghosts*
8. JONATHAN SWIFT · *A Modest Proposal*
9. *Three Tang Dynasty Poets*
10. WALT WHITMAN · *On the Beach at Night Alone*
11. KENKŌ · *A Cup of Sake Beneath the Cherry Trees*
12. BALTASAR GRACIÁN · *How to Use Your Enemies*
13. JOHN KEATS · *The Eve of St Agnes*
14. THOMAS HARDY · *Woman much missed*
15. GUY DE MAUPASSANT · *Femme Fatale*
16. MARCO POLO · *Travels in the Land of Serpents and Pearls*
17. SUETONIUS · *Caligula*
18. APOLLONIUS OF RHODES · *Jason and Medea*
19. ROBERT LOUIS STEVENSON · *Olalla*
20. KARL MARX AND FRIEDRICH ENGELS · *The Communist Manifesto*
21. PETRONIUS · *Trimalchio's Feast*
22. JOHANN PETER HEBEL · *How a Ghastly Story Was Brought to Light by a Common or Garden Butcher's Dog*
23. HANS CHRISTIAN ANDERSEN · *The Tinder Box*
24. RUDYARD KIPLING · *The Gate of the Hundred Sorrows*
25. DANTE · *Circles of Hell*
26. HENRY MAYHEW · *Of Street Piemen*
27. HAFEZ · *The nightingales are drunk*
28. GEOFFREY CHAUCER · *The Wife of Bath*
29. MICHEL DE MONTAIGNE · *How We Weep and Laugh at the Same Thing*
30. THOMAS NASHE · *The Terrors of the Night*
31. EDGAR ALLAN POE · *The Tell-Tale Heart*
32. MARY KINGSLEY · *A Hippo Banquet*
33. JANE AUSTEN · *The Beautifull Cassandra*
34. ANTON CHEKHOV · *Gooseberries*
35. SAMUEL TAYLOR COLERIDGE · *Well, they are gone, and here must I remain*
36. JOHANN WOLFGANG VON GOETHE · *Sketchy, Doubtful, Incomplete Jottings*
37. CHARLES DICKENS · *The Great Winglebury Duel*
38. HERMAN MELVILLE · *The Maldive Shark*
39. ELIZABETH GASKELL · *The Old Nurse's Story*
40. NIKOLAY LESKOV · *The Steel Flea*

41. HONORÉ DE BALZAC · *The Atheist's Mass*
42. CHARLOTTE PERKINS GILMAN · *The Yellow Wall-Paper*
43. C.P. CAVAFY · *Remember, Body . . .*
44. FYODOR DOSTOEVSKY · *The Meek One*
45. GUSTAVE FLAUBERT · *A Simple Heart*
46. NIKOLAI GOGOL · *The Nose*
47. SAMUEL PEPYS · *The Great Fire of London*
48. EDITH WHARTON · *The Reckoning*
49. HENRY JAMES · *The Figure in the Carpet*
50. WILFRED OWEN · *Anthem For Doomed Youth*
51. WOLFGANG AMADEUS MOZART · *My Dearest Father*
52. PLATO · *Socrates' Defence*
53. CHRISTINA ROSSETTI · *Goblin Market*
54. *Sindbad the Sailor*
55. SOPHOCLES · *Antigone*
56. RYŪNOSUKE AKUTAGAWA · *The Life of a Stupid Man*
57. LEO TOLSTOY · *How Much Land Does A Man Need?*
58. GIORGIO VASARI · *Leonardo da Vinci*
59. OSCAR WILDE · *Lord Arthur Savile's Crime*
60. SHEN FU · *The Old Man of the Moon*
61. AESOP · *The Dolphins, the Whales and the Gudgeon*
62. MATSUO BASHŌ · *Lips too Chilled*
63. EMILY BRONTË · *The Night is Darkening Round Me*
64. JOSEPH CONRAD · *To-morrow*
65. RICHARD HAKLUYT · *The Voyage of Sir Francis Drake Around the Whole Globe*
66. KATE CHOPIN · *A Pair of Silk Stockings*
67. CHARLES DARWIN · *It was snowing butterflies*
68. BROTHERS GRIMM · *The Robber Bridegroom*
69. CATULLUS · *I Hate and I Love*
70. HOMER · *Circe and the Cyclops*
71. D. H. LAWRENCE · *Il Duro*
72. KATHERINE MANSFIELD · *Miss Brill*
73. OVID · *The Fall of Icarus*
74. SAPPHO · *Come Close*
75. IVAN TURGENEV · *Kasyan from the Beautiful Lands*
76. VIRGIL · *O Cruel Alexis*
77. H. G. WELLS · *A Slip under the Microscope*
78. HERODOTUS · *The Madness of Cambyses*
79. *Speaking of Siva*
80. *The Dhammapada*